T0198557

IN DEFENSE
OF THE
UNBORN

JOURNEY FROM WOMB TO TOMB

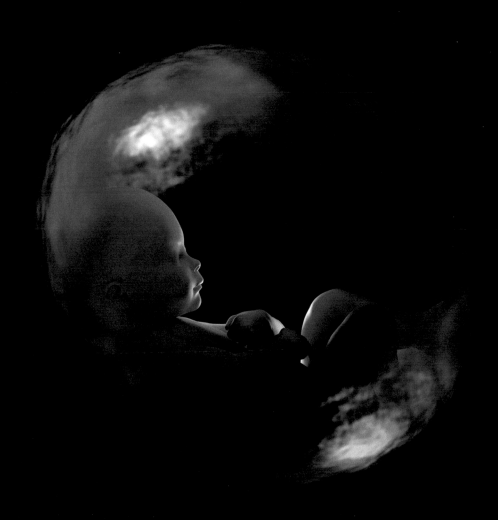

ERNESTO Y. LEE, M.D.

Copyright © 2020 by Ernesto Y. Lee, M.D. 820932

All rights reserved. No part of this book may be reproduced
or transmitted in any form or by any means, electronic or
mechanical, including photocopying, recording, or by any
information storage and retrieval system, without permission
in writing from the copyright owner.

To order additional copies of this book, contact:
Xlibris
844-714-8691
www.Xlibris.com
Orders@Xlibris.com

ISBN: Softcover   978-1-6641-3529-1
         Hardcover   978-1-6641-3530-7
         EBook   978-1-6641-3528-4

Print information available on the last page

Rev. date: 10/06/2020

CONTENTS

INTRODUCTION

THE LAUNCHING OF this book is in response to the increasing number and popularity of abortion not only in America but all over the world. It is hoped that by bringing this subject to the attention of the general public, millions will be saved in terms of the mighty dollars and human lives, more especially the unborn.

Although at first glance the Malthusian Theory which asserts that Calamities, War and Famine are necessary evils to control the population of the earth may seem a better alternative to using abortion as we know it to carry out this objective, having experienced myself and survived the evils of calamities, hunger, and diseases during World War II, I vehemently reject these contentions, which should never be condoned for any reason in a civilized world. And though it seems that all is fair at war with both opposing parties armed with their best weapons it is ***never fair in abortion where the helpless unborn baby is a sitting duck target with no chance or choice to evade or fight back.***

To live life to its fullest is a dream we all aspire. To reward ourselves with the fruits of our own labor is a noble end, but to share our rewards with the rest of the world is even much nobler and worthy of our endeavor; for there is nothing more rewarding than to leave this world better than we found it.

CHAPTER I

THE SANCTITY OF LIFE

1. When does life begin and when does it end?
2. Why is killing an adult person a crime and killing a fetus or newborn infant (Infanticide) not a crime?

THESE ARE THE two compelling questions that inspired me to write about the Sanctity of Life and the purpose of living.

The answer to the first question is that *life begins at conception,* i.e. *with the successful union of the egg and the sperm.* It does not matter if the fertilized egg is 1 day old in the womb or 1 day after birth. Life is life no matter how old or whether or not it is inside the womb.

To borrow from Shakespeare's work "What is in a name that we call a rose which by any name will smell as sweet;"so is infanticide, which by any name is murder of the first degree that results in a dead innocent, infant, no matter how or where it is done, is the answer to my second question. It ends the life of a human being regardless if it is a fetus, an infant, or a child.

Justice is blind. It must be applied equally to all, regardless of age, color or sex. And Justice has long been denied to the infants or newborns and it is time to change our laws to deliver justice for all.

ABORTION is defined by Webster as the expulsion of the human fetus within the first 12 weeks of pregnancy before it is viable. In layman's language, it is a termination of pregnancy by human intervention at any term, early or late term, regardless of the viability of the fetus. It can be criminal or therapeutic to save a mother's life like, for example, in a case of premature placental separation with severe bleeding which can be fatal if nothing is done.

From the perspective of anybody who has a conscience, no one person is that important or indispensable as to justify the taking away of one's life to save another life. If the fetus dies in the process of saving the mother, whether or not the decision to intervene is justified, judgment is better left in the hands of God.

The pro-choice advocates continue to practice abortion under the guise of it being a constitutional right of a person to do whatsoever she wants to do with her own body. But to counter this point, when a woman decides to become pregnant, she no longer is alone in her own body. She becomes an obligatory custodian of another human being who has the same constitutional right to life and liberty as she. She cannot claim self-defense because the fetus is not attacking her. In fact, it is not the fetus' fault that put her in this condition. She only has herself to blame for this unwanted pregnancy which is the tantalizing envy of so many other childless couples.

Of course there is always an exception to the rules. A great disagreement exists between those who believe in making a pregnancy by incest or rape an exception and would justify abortion, against those who stick to their guns with the antiabortion side in a debate where there is no winner.

Another rationalization of abortion is that since rape and abortion have been in existence since the beginning of time, we therefore cannot reasonably change these heinous acts in our time anymore. If both acts are considered sinful in our culture, does it mean then that to commit sin to correct another sin is justified? Let our conscience be the judge.

According to the teachings of the Catholic Church, life is a creation of God and must be protected and kept sacred at all costs by all means at any age and circumstance. Simply speaking, we assume that *life begins at birth. But biologically speaking, however, it is our consensus that life begins at conception i.e., after the successful union of a woman's egg and a man's lucky sperm or group of sperms.*

If, for example, only one sperm can penetrate the barrier and impregnate one egg, the resulting fertilization will produce a single pregnancy; if two sperms impregnate an egg the resulting fertilization will produce a twin pregnancy; and so on up to a certain limit. The fertilized egg then travels from the ovary through the fallopian tube to the uterus where implantation in the lining of the uterus takes place and pregnancy begins. It is a common practice to count the age of pregnancy to begin from the first day of the last menstrual period or cycle of a woman and ends at 39 - 40 weeks, the EDC (Expected Date of Confinement).

By the time we are born, each one of us has already been pre-determined to be a distinct individual with unique personality traits, idiosyncrasies, instincts, conscience, characteristics, etc. Amazingly, but by no means accidentally, of the thousands who are born each day all over the world, no two persons exactly look alike.

Even twins are not mirror image or carbon copies of each other. They have identifying marks that distinguish one from the other. How we arrive at our destination depends upon several factors: the genes we are born with; the opportunities and obstacles we encounter; and our passion and tenacity to reach our goal, which is to live life to its fullest and eventual demise as designed by our Maker. Of course, as the dogma of the Catholic Church tells us, this is in addition to the main reason for our creation, which is to *Know God and to Love Him.*

In deference to the graying members of our society, old people will be referred to here as retirees to spare them from being unpleasantly stereotyped or stigmatized as rotten, spoiled, deteriorated, over-ripe, stale, dilapidated, or has-been.

CHAPTER II

GROWING OLD VS. GROWING UP

TO *GROW OLD* and to *grow up* are entirely two different "breeds of same feather". The former, also called *senescence* or aging, is a natural biological process of deterioration that begins at conception, characterized by graying of the hair; forgetfulness; stiffness and soreness of the joints; skin wrinkles, senile spots; sexual decline or dysfunction, etc.; while *growing up* is a psycho-social and upgraded behavioral transformation that evolves from education and training; enhanced further according to how friendly or hostile the environment will be encountered.

If we live long enough, each one is entitled to a happy, golden retirement; but to retire in style is an opportunity and privilege not everyone can attain or afford. It requires a life time of preparation and planning, starting with a good fortune and favorable family background and support; and fine-tuned further by good education and discipline. Unfortunately, even a simple retirement is beyond the reach of some poor or underprivileged and uneducated segment of our population, who must continue to labor and earn a living till he no longer is able, due to sickness and debility or till he dies of old age.

To elucidate our understanding of the intricacies or complexities of life, let me walk you through the transition from *womb to tomb*. As already stated earlier, ordinarily we speak of life to begin at birth. This is probably one of the reasons why some people like the pro-choice advocates and the uneducated or uninformed do not view abortion (*termination of life of the unborn*) as infanticide or murder of an innocent baby, since there is yet no palpable life involved outside a mother's womb; and therefore they do not suffer any guilt feelings of the crime.

Some may not be necessarily evil people who snap life at the budding stage of development for only one good reason: to save the mother's life. Biologically speaking however, as mentioned earlier, life begins at conception, which *now has a soul and therefore sacred*. It is this writer's stance, that there is never a justification to take away one's life to save another. The unborn baby's life is just as sacred as the mother's life in the eyes of God who created us.

CHAPTER III

USING ABORTION AS A TOOL IN SEX SELECTION AND BIRTH CONTROL

THANKS TO OUR advanced knowledge in medical science and technology, we can now tell when life, as we know it, begins and determine the sex of the fetus in the mother's womb as early as fourteen weeks old, using the ultra sound machine. Unfortunately, this sophisticated technology has become a convenient tool by some Godless people to select the sex of their unborn babies and discard the ones they do not want. Even worse, some couples who apparently have no conscience are using abortion as a form of birth control, instead of using acceptable preventive measures like the birth control pills or the rhythm method; unmindful of the fact that *every abortion implies the taking away of life and liberty of an innocent human being.*

As blatantly detestable and gruesome as it is to know that harvested organs from aborted fetuses are being sold for whatever purposes in the black market, there is even a worse and disgustingly shocking and abhor able revelation going around in some poor parts of the world that children are being kidnapped and slaughtered to harvest their organs for sale in the black market.

At this stage of gestation, it is difficult to tell for sure if the fetus can already subjectively feel the same kind of pain as we do. One would think that there is no safer place on earth than to be in a mother's womb, with all the protection and cushion available to him or her. But the truth is that, sad to say, no baby is safe inside the mother's womb in the hands of the criminal abortionist with all his armamentarium to terminate a baby's life. Even if the baby survives after being suctioned out from its apparently safe haven, she or he can still be exterminated by the abortionist if the mother so decides; like in the case of a failed late term abortion in Virginia. As explained by the Democratic governor, the protocol only requires that the helpless new born be made comfortable after delivery, but is then deprived of any life support later and is just allowed to expire on its own.

It is interesting to note here by the same token, which appeared in the news, that a certain senator from Illinois made history by casting the deciding vote that deprived a newborn of his life and liberty at a staff meeting wherein it was debated whether or not to give the usual life support to a baby that unexpectedly survived a botched late term abortion. The nays won and the baby was discarded with the dirty linen into the bin to terminate its life.

As horrible and deplorable as this Late Term Abortion appears to be, it is heartening to hear from the President's State of the Union Address that he will sign into law as soon as a new bill reaches his desk, which will **out- law Late Term Abortion.**

Another gratifying new information for the prolife and unborn alike, that has been circulating recently, is that more states are outlawing outright abortion,(not only Late Term Abortion) Texas now being number eight state on the list.

The new bill called *The Abortion Survivor Bill* mandates that a baby that survives an abortion is entitled to receive the same life support as any other human being in a similar situation.

At four to six weeks of pregnancy, the fetal heart begins to beat. From here on the baby continues to develop to be a human being with a soul until full term at 40 weeks or 9 months. A baby has to be at least 5 weeks of gestational age to survive outside the mother's womb. The babies that are born before 37 weeks are considered premature and require extraordinary care to remain alive. Those that survive late term abortion and abnormalities secondary to drug abuse by the mother during pregnancy, especially the first trimester, may still face many different kinds of hazard in a new cruel world; which is full of infectious diseases, drug addiction, and gang violence. This is where good family upbringing really counts. I can only still remember my own son when he was in high school where he became an outcast from his friends simply because he refused to join them in their smoking and drinking sprees.

But as designed by our Creator, the majority of us do survive to reach adulthood unscathed to live life to its fullest; and on to a happy, golden retirement, which is the best time to live. But unfortunately, golden age is not always that luminous as pure gold; and before I begin my *lament to old age*, allow me first to divert for a short time from our itinerary to recollect and share with you here some of my most memorable and rewarding personal experiences related to the issue of abortion which was legalized by the U.S. Supreme Court in 1973.

CHAPTER IV

A SHORT DIVERSION FROM OUR ITINERARY

BACK IN THE Philippines in the late 60s where I practiced General Surgery and Family Medicine prior to returning to America in the early 70s, I was pleasantly surprised by an embrace from somebody I never met before, sincerely saying, "thank you very much, Doc, for my life. I would not be here today if not because of you." My jaw dropped, mumbling to myself "what did I do to deserve this credit?" Then he said with a calming smile, "I am the one you saved inside my mother's womb which was mistakenly diagnosed as a tumor and scheduled to be surgically removed by another doctor. You made the second opinion, cancelled the surgery, and allowed the pregnancy to proceed till you delivered her successfully. So, as my mother kept telling this story time and time again, the more I got increasingly curious and eagerly interested to meet you in person." One seldom hears this kind of story about himself, and certainly this one made my day. Without further hesitation, I said to him, "Thank God, not me. I am only His instrument." And he said, "And you, too," in a grateful tone.

Subsequently in another unforgettable and happy occasion, I was pleasantly greeted by my previous patient in a restaurant in Chandler, AZ, saying," I can never thank you enough, Doc, for giving me my son. He is now studying to be an engineer at ASU."Then one thing led to another, and I remembered this woman who came to me some years ago in great emotional turmoil and crying because of her unplanned pregnancy, which she could hardly afford at that time.

I had just finished my routine follow-up examination of the babies of two beautiful teen-aged mothers whose pregnancies I had saved earlier with my timely and God-inspired counseling – and now this patient. My hands were full, so it seemed at the moment, and there was nothing more I could do. But I knew I had a mission to accomplish and therefore I had to continue trying to salvage as many unwanted pregnancies as they came to my attention and care.

I just could not help admiring in silence those babies as I was doing their physical examination. "What an awful waste of valuable and beautiful lives if their mothers had gone to the wrong hands!" I kept saying to myself. So, using all the power of persuasion and supplication that was within me, I showed her a list of professional people waiting and wanting to adopt a baby, as an alternative. Thankfully, there was a sudden change in the tone of her voice and in an instant she muttered, "Thank you for your advice, Doc, I will go on with this pregnancy and keep the baby for myself instead;" keeping in the back of her mind the possibility of giving it up for adoption in case the winds of change would turn for the worse against her favor, financially and emotionally.

I breathed a sigh of triumph and relief, realizing what I had just accomplished; and thanking her at the same time for listening, and for taking my advice; thus making me so happy indeed. To feel happy is something we normally experience in life now and then; but to feel happy, knowing that we have just saved another precious life is something we can never put a price tag on. And I just thank God for giving me the privilege and opportunity to take care of one of His most beautiful and precious creations: *life itself.*

A mother probably does not realize or see what a big mistake she has committed until she has seen the survivor of an unwanted pregnancy. I can only imagine how the biological parents of the two adopted boys of my daughter will feel if they can only see how great their children are doing now. The older one, a red-head American from a single mother in Ohio, now ten years old, is very bright and very handsome with dimples. The younger one, now eight, from a China orphanage, is also very bright and good looking after having two plastic procedures for his double cleft lip and palate. Serving as altar boys in their church on Sundays, both are excellent students; and show a great promise of a bright future.

Watching these boys grow up is really fun and amusing. One day the younger boy was crying after being bullied by the older boy and their mother tried to pacify the little boy saying, "Stop crying Raphy, you are now OK." "No I am not OK because I am still crying," he immediately responded. We were rather stunned to hear this kind of reasoning from a four-year boy who never spoke one word of English when he first came to America at age two. Then in another occasion, he impressed me with another surprise. Watching me struggling to get up from my wheelchair, he gave me a warm embrace on my waist saying, "Grandpa, next time you need help, you let me know, OK?" And he would never part until I said OK.

Not to be outdone, Gabriel, the older boy then six years old, after seeing me struggling to walk in the hall way of the care home when he came to visit, hurried to bring me my wheel chair which was parked 4 tables away saying, "Here Grandpa, don't fall down again," knowing I have had several falls before.

In another display of talent, Gabriel, then six years old, saved his mother a traffic violation ticket when she got caught by the cop for not making a complete stop at a stop sign. From out of the blue Gabriel, who was in the back seat blurted, "Officer, We are from Louisville. We are just visiting our grandpa who is sick in the hospital." The officer who was starting to write a ticket just melted and slowly withdrew is gadget from the window and said "OK, just drive carefully next time". Amazing indeed, these boys, as young as they are - already paying back to their benefactors the care and love they get.

As hard as it is to surmise how their biological parents will react to realize what they had lost or given away for nothing, it is even harder not to assume that they would want back these precious boys for themselves. They would most likely just be consoled, however, with the knowledge that their loss is somebody else's gain by Devine Providence.

Figure 1 Raphael 8 and Gabriel 10 with Ampy and Chris Cogswell, adoptive parents

Another lucky survivor of abortion is one whom I personally know. When her mother was three months pregnant, her obstetrician wanted to do an amniocentesis to confirm or rule-out a suspected "Down's Syndrome," more commonly called Mongoloid, the reason being that her abdominal ultrasound at this time showed some abnormality in the umbilical cord that is a common finding in Down's syndrome.

Figure 2 Christine with blue guitar with the Midnight Angels Band

Her father, a very devout Catholic, objected saying "What for? Even if the baby is a Mongoloid, my wife and I will never consider an abortion," which would have been the next routinely recommended step if confirmed. "We will gladly accept whatever God will give us." And fortunately the pregnancy, after being blessed by a Regnum Christi priest, proceeded uneventfully; and the baby turned out to be a very smart and beautiful girl, who now is a championship-contender ice skater; pop singer in Hollywood; ballet dancer; piano and bass guitar player; Tae Kwando black belter; and very bright. How many fathers and babies are this lucky? Only God knows.

Figure 3 Christine Lee Ballet Dancer

Figure 4 Christine, Ice Skater

Chapter V

TO DISPENSE OR NOT TO DISPENSE THE ABORTION PILLS

T O SAY NO to a request for abortion pills to a casual acquaintance or a stranger is by far a lot easier to do than to a close friend or relative. I will be remiss in my recollection if I fail to mention here my last temptation to dispense, which I found to be one of the hardest to overcome.

This dear friend asked me if I could give his three-month pregnant extramarital girlfriend an abortion pill. Thank God, I was able to muster all the courage to say no at a difficult time and to give the right advice. The pregnancy proceeded uneventfully, and to the happiness of all concerned, when she grew up, she turned out to be very smart woman who is now a professional care giver.

CHAPTER VI

CHILDREN ADOPTION CENTER

A T THIS POINT in time, I thought to myself, how nice and appropriate would it be if there was a government sponsored crisis center or *Children adoption Center* where lost or confused pregnant women in emotional turmoil and financial need like the preceding patients I cited above can turn to and get counseling and help; instead of going straight to Planned Parenthood or abortion clinics where they most likely will end up having an abortion.

People in this situation do not think straight. They are desperate and helpless, and will just accept whatever advice or remedy they can get to help them out of the bind they are in or extricate them from their seemingly insurmountable dilemma. Based upon my own personal observation and experience, it is my considered opinion that a vast majority of these kinds of patients, under ordinary circumstances, normally do not really mean or intend to kill their babies.

Yet, when put in a situation where they are made to believe or understand that there is no other way or that the best way out of their predicament is abortion, they will just blindly do or accept anything against their will or choice. This is where sound psychological and medical counseling is direly needed. Such timely counseling or service will surely save millions of unborn babies from being exterminated. It will also help reduce the number of postpartum psychosis and obviate guilt feelings and regrets on the part of the helpless mothers for years to come – even to eternity.

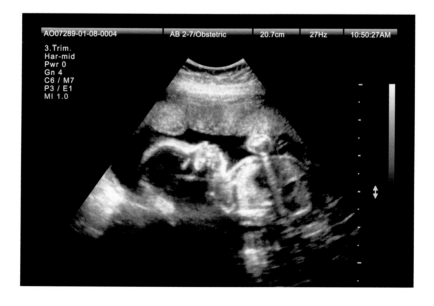

Figure 5 3rd Trimester Ultrasound

CHAPTER VII

THE ABDOMINAL ULTRASOUND LAW OF KENTUCKY

I N THIS COUNTRY, it is illegal to show to a prospective abortion patient her abdominal ultrasound for the sole purpose of turning her off from proceeding with the abortion once she sees the image of her baby inside her womb so full of life and kicking; and whose umbilical cord, the lifeline, is about to be cut off.

So far, Kentucky is the only state in the nation to this date that I know of to legalize the showing of such abdominal ultra sound to the expectant woman who is about to have an abortion. This *Ultra Sound Law* which had been earlier contested by the ACLU was only recently legalized by the U.S. Supreme Court-unquestionably a great victory for the Pro Life proponents.

It will certainly be a welcome move and a gift from God if other states will follow suit, now that the Supreme Court is filling up with more conservative justices under President Trump. Such a move will surely save millions more babies, unbeknownst to the public.

Figure 6 L - R Andre, Christine, Chita, Ernesto Sr., Lysette, Raphael, Ampy, Chris Cogswell, Gabriel, Delailah and Ernesto, Jr., parents of Christine Lee

CHAPTER VIII

OUR FIRST CHILDHOOD

NOW-GOING BACK TO our first childhood. When we are babies we are spoon-fed. We eat on a silver platter. When we cry for any reason anytime, our mother is always there to pacify us with her milk and warm embrace – oftentimes with a sweet lullaby that we will always remember.

When we are uncomfortable because our diaper is soiled and wet our mother is always there to change it. Life is care free and we have nothing to worry about. We are abound with toys, hugs, and kisses from our loved ones.

CHAPTER IX

OUR SECOND CHILDHOOD

BUT NOT SO in our second childhood, which usually starts in as early as in our 70s or our 80s and beyond. From childhood and up until our 60's or early 70's it seems like life as we know it will never change or end. We eat whatever we like, without any restrictions; or do anything as we please. But time flies so fast that before we realize, our youth is gone.

Girls grow up so fast they change their toys for boys in a whirlwind of passion and romance; and boys change their toy guns for real guns in a whirlwind of fantasy and imagination. Before we realize, our earning and accumulating days are over and spending time is here. This is where good education and adequate good financial planning for the future really count.

Now - going back to abortion. One good news that just came out recently is that the Secretary of Health and Human Resources just announced to the UN that it is the policy of this administration that there is no international right to abortion and that our tax money should not be used to fund abortion facilities like the Planned Parenthood clinics.

This is with the *Imprimatur* of President Trump, who reiterated his pro-life stance when he said that every child is a gift from God and must be kept sacred and protected all the time.

CHAPTER X

EMERGENCY FUND FOR UNPLANNED PREGNANCIES

ANOTHER ALTERNATIVE TO abortion that I strongly support is the availability of an Emergency Fund to aid such unplanned and unaffordable pregnancies, not only to helpless, single mothers in emotional distress; but also to distraught, married mothers who are financially strapped and thereby unable to make the right decision. There is no doubt that adoptive parents, who are in a position to do so, are more than willing to chip in their share if only to exercise their Christian opportunity to help and assure their chance of having a baby to adopt in their time frame.

CHAPTER XI

LAMENT TO OLD AGE

H AVING SURVIVED THE rigors of youth and growing up we now enter the shadow of old age. The life style we live depends upon our financial and health status. Then in our 70s or early 80s we hardly notice the change but the vigor and flame of youth have faded away and are now gone. We are now at the receiving end of the stick. We are at the mercy of people around us for anything we need, including bathing and dressing at times, if we are now debilitated or disabled.

When we spill food on our clothes or on the floor we get a sermon for being clumsy; when we spill coffee on the table or the floor we receive an instant order to clean it up; lucky are we if don't get desegregated at the dining table and have to eat in a separate low table alone, using only wooden bowls because we have dropped and broken too many China plates; when we turn on the TV volume too loud because now we are hard of hearing, we get a louder order to turn it down; our Insurance premium goes higher and higher because we have gotten too many tickets from car accidents or moving violations, etc.

Life gets increasingly frustrating as we grow older, but life must go on and we have to cope with the new demands of living. Such is what we call the many faces of existence and aging.

CHAPTER XII

NEW ABORTION LAW IN CALIFORNIA

NOT TO BE sidelined or outdone in the field of abortion is the state of California which recently passed a law requiring the State Universities to provide upon request abortion pills to students who are pregnant, to keep them from cutting classes or dropping out of school.

There is no hesitation in my mind to predict the reaction of the only president in modern times who is not shy or afraid to lay his anti-abortion card on the table. Would it be the lesser of two evils and less expensive just to provide them with birth control pills instead? To spend our tax money to kill babies is another questionable issue on morality that the pro-life president is being blamed for by the ultra-left liberals.

Will the famous evangelist Billy Graham, who has recently expressed his dissatisfaction of President Trump and his withdrawal of his support of him, continue to preach Christianity, which by virtue of its mandate is inherently and naturally anti-abortion?

CHAPTER XIII

THE GRAYING FOR AMERICA

WITH THE EVER increasing advance in medical science and improved living style and condition, more and more are living longer, resulting in the *Graying of America*. Of interest to note is the most recent statistics that showed the average life span in America has increased to 78 years old. It is therefore imperative that provisions be made early in life to avoid being destitute or impoverished in our retirement years. The Bureau of Labor statistics further showed that people who like their jobs and continue working past their retirement years live longer than those who do otherwise.

A good paying job or a profitable business is a desirable start in our journey toward retirement, but neither does guarantee the desired adequate savings that we will need. It is not what we earn but what we save is what counts. There is no magic wand that can tell us exactly how much we need in retirement. It is therefore advisable or imperative to set aside regularly a fixed percentage of one's earnings to assure a good and comfortable nest egg in retirement.

CHAPTER XIV

SIGNS OF OLD AGE DETERIORATION AND DEMENTIA

LUCKILY FOR THE majority of us, having survived extermination by abortion, now in our old age, we realize we can no longer carry a bagful of flour or a bucketful of water as easily as years ago. Our joints get stiffer and achy and sometimes are squeaky. Our knees are prune to buckle and we trip easily even on tiny obstacles. We look for our eye glasses everywhere in the house when they are parked on our foreheads.

We go to the garage to get or do something, and once there we do not know or remember what we went there for. After we have driven one or two blocks away from our house, we suddenly turn around to make sure we have closed the garage door; we search all over the rooms in the house to look for the car keys that we have left in the pocket of one of our pants or jacket; the words that we want to say do not come out of our mouth spontaneously but stay at the tip of our tongue; our mates would tell us to list down what we need to do, but still we go to the kitchen to get a cup of ice tea only to come back to the dining table with a piece of toast without butter; we make several trips to the kitchen for a cup of coffee because we have forgotten we already had one or two earlier; we keep repeating ourselves in conversations because we have forgotten what we have said earlier, etc.

As if these are not enough to make us mad and miserable, we look at the mirror and see we have a turkey neck; we see wrinkles on our cheeks what were once smooth and rosy; our midsection protrudes and we attribute it to our middle age or too much beer. We cannot eat as much as we want because we are weight watching; we cannot eat much sweet because we are diabetic; we have to cut down on our salt because we have high blood pressure; we want to eat roast pork, but we have to cut down eating fats because we have high cholesterol, etc. There are so many don'ts in our second childhood, or even more sometimes, than there were in our first childhood; thus, making life at this point in time not worth living anymore.

Our brain deteriorates as we grow older, but to exhibit forgetfulness in extremes is something else and worrisome. It can be the beginning of Alzheimer's disease. Woo to the mate of a couple who can no longer recognize the other and vice versa. If one cannot find his way home, going thru the same route for years to and from the grocery or the church; this is of grave concern, which requires immediate medical attention.

The preceding are just some of the early signs of deterioration and dementia that can only get worse as we continue to live to our golden age.

Now we have a new set of vocabularies, too: heart burns, insomnia, constipation, diarrhea, back and joint pains and stiffness; suppository, enema, cane, wheelchair, high blood pressure, diabetes, shortness of breath, chest pain, blurred vision or cataract, etc. In addition, if we are privileged, we now speak the language of the elite, like Investment, Wall Street Journal, Common Stocks; Mutual Funds, Dow Jones, Annuity, Treasury Bills, 401K, SP500,etc.

When I was young I used to pray to God to give me a long life and now that I have it, with all the attendant and unpleasant things that come with it, I have my second thoughts about long life without good health. The longer I am retired, the more I am getting tired.

Unable to drive anymore because of my Guillain-Barre Syndrome, with my hands and feet still numb after many years, I feel like a prisoner in my own home. I thought that when I retired I would be able to do all the things I wanted to do in my younger days, only to find out that anything I do now is a big hassle and energy exhausting. Let alone the fact that I have to take 20 pills a day to remain alive. The things that used to fascinate me in my youth are no longer fascinating.

I often wonder how those old people many generations ago passed their time without the modern amenities that we now enjoy -the radios, TVs, sporty cars, airplanes, Internet, etc. Yet they lived and contributed to this world their talents and innovations that transformed this world into a new world of unlimited amenities, recreations, and comforts that we now enjoy and cannot live without. Also, the longer I live, the longer my list of friends and relatives that I pray for grows; and the lesser number of friends I have left to socialize with and eventually attend my funeral if I am lucky to outlive them.

CHAPTER XV

NOT ALL THAT'S OLD IS BAD

BUT NOT ALL that is old is bad. I still love to see old familiar faces and places; old friends and old songs or melodies that bring back old memories of yesterday when I was young, vibrant, and productive, etc. Growing old is no fun, but I thank God for giving me the wisdom of old age. I can negotiate the curves, the sharp corners, and barriers on the road of life a lot easier than when I was young.

As I approach closer to my finishing line, I look back with gratitude for all I have had and enjoyed in life. I thank God for giving me 2 wonderful, beautiful children; 5 wonderful, beautiful grandchildren and a good, faithful wife. If I have a chance to live my life all over again, I will surely be glad to take the same path. With God on my side, I certainly have nothing to fear.

Now – continuing in our journey toward retirement which is just one step closer to our final destination - the tomb. Lucky are we who approach retirement well prepared and grow old together with our spouses to a happy retirement, for as they say, "old age is a lonely time to spend life alone;"but it is also the best time to live if we have enough savings and income.

The life style we live is determined by the financial preparation we have made in our accumulation years, which are best in our 30s or 40s and on to our 50s.We just have to make sure, like they say, we "don't run out of money before we run out of time", i.e., we don't outlive our savings. How we withdraw and spend our savings will be an important part of the equation of our life style and wealth preservation. Our pension, our Social Security, IRA, and Investment Earnings will need the utmost and careful management by ourselves; or per advice of qualified and reliable financial advisers like Vanguard, Fidelity, Ave Maria, PIMCO, etc. if we arc unablc to do so ourselves.

We must also remember how hard we worked to accumulate our wealth, and passing it to the right heirs at the right time is just as important as accumulating it. By and large, the above problem may seem to belong only to the privileged or well-endowed retiree. On the other hand, however, it can also be a hurdle for the underprivileged or poor retiree who lives only on his social security income, no matter how small, granting he has one. More on the brighter side, the poor retiree can be just as happy and contented with what he has, enjoying life living at his level.

We must also remember to be kind to our heirs or successors to spare them the trouble of having to dig through rubbles of antiquated documents or records that have gathered dusts in the cabinets or drawers by sorting them out while we are still of sound minds; or spare them the agony of having to fight among themselves or in court if we neglect to have a Will or Trust.

It is not fair to pass our wealth to undeserving and ungrateful heirs like one of my patients who never came to visit his father in the nursing home more than once a year; but when his father died, he instantly appeared to collect his share of the inheritance.

Chapter XVI

UPPER CLASS SCOTTSDALE SENIOR CENTER

WHILE MOST OF the members at this upper class Scottsdale Senior Center belong to the elite class, some of those I come in contact with, some of them Snow Birds, may not be really as wealthy as they look, but they seem to be the ones who come prepared for this journey and enjoying life, well dressed and well-manicured, in their retirement years.

With their houses all paid off and no more children to support in college, life goes smoothly and happily for them, doing the ballroom dancing once or twice a week for socialization and physical therapy or exercise; dining at their favorite restaurants; visiting the casinos now and then, etc. This is in sharp contrast to the living style of the less fortunate who must continue to labor till they run out of gas.

CHAPTER XVII

A TIME TO DECIDE WHEN AND WHERE TO RETIRE

NOW IN THE sunset of our lives and nearing the end of our journey, it is also time to make a decision if and when we are ready and where to retire. Others who are deeply rooted where they are because of family ties or relationships and business commitments will stay put. But before I proceed any further, I wish to make it clear here that it is neither my intention nor is it within the realm of this book to give financial advice or tell prospective retirees when and where to retire.

Those who prefer to move elsewhere will have several factors to consider:

A. THE WEATHER.

Those who love the snow and cold weather will certainly settle down in the Eastern states, like Minnesota, Wisconsin, Massachusetts, etc. For those who love the sunshine and long summer heat will settle in the Western states like Arizona and New Mexico. Other amenities and attractions for consideration are the presence of golf courses, parks, hunting and fishing grounds, age restricted communities, etc.

B. Living and Health Care Condition:

Good health and good sanitation are an essential part of good living. Good churches, medical facilities, and good doctors are desirable; and play an important part in our decision to pick where to retire, especially, for those who have health conditions that cannot tolerate the cold weather and air pollution. The proximity to the airport, good taxi and bus transportation services, good movie houses, excellent restaurants, groceries, etc. are an added attraction to our choice of where to live.

C. Tax Implication.

For the well-endowed retirees, taxes will not be a big issue, but for the less fortunate ones, the presence or absence of state tax, sales tax, property tax, social security tax, Inheritance tax, etc. will need to be addressed before making a decision.

At present, there are only four states that have no sales tax:

1. Oregon

2. New Hampshire

3. Montana

4. Delaware.

Only Hawaii has an excise tax that is equivalent to a sales tax, which at 4%, puts it as the lowest sales tax in the nation. Tennessee, at 9.4% has the highest sales tax. The average local sales tax rates in the nation range from 5.36% to 9.47%.

D. Inheritance Tax or Estate Tax Exemption.

This is the lowest amount below which the estate does not pay a tax. Recently, the Federal Estate Tax exemption was raised to $11.4 million. While other states usually follow the Federal guide lines in lowering their exemption tax, it is important to note that Massachusetts and Oregon have the lowest estate tax exemption at $1,000,000, which makes it least attractive even to the wealthy retirees.

According to some survey in the Internet, states are classified according to how tax friendly they are.

Very Tax Friendly:

Tax wise, the following states are the best to retire in: They have no State tax, and have no Tax on Retirement Income:

1. Alaska

2. Florida

3. Georgia

4. Mississippi

5. Nevada,

6. South Dakota

7. Wyoming

II. Tax Friendly:

No Tax on Social Security Income and other retirement Income:

1. Alabama

2. Arkansas

3. Colorado

4. Delaware

5. Idaho

6. Illinois

7. Kentucky

8. Louisiana

9. Michigan,

10. New Hampshire

11. Oklahoma,

12. Pennsylvania,

13. South Carolina,

14. Tennessee,

15. Texas,

16. Virginia,

17. Washington

18. West Virginia.

III. Moderately Tax Friendly:

States that offer smaller tax deductions on some form of retirement Income, sales, property, and estate tax:

1. New Jersey,

2. 2. New Mexico,

3. 3. Arizona,

4. 4. D.C.,

5. Hawaii,

6. Indiana,

7. Iowa,

8. Kansas,

9. Maryland,

10. Massachusetts,

11. Missouri,

12. Montana,

13. New York,

14. North Carolina,

15. North Dakota,

16. Ohio,

17. Oregon,

18. Utah

19. Wisconsin.

IV Not Tax Friendly:

The following states that offer minimal or no retirement income tax benefits:

1. California

2. Connecticut

3. Maine

4. Minnesota

5. Nebraska

6. Rhode Island

7. Vermont

CHAPTER **XVIII**

AGE RESTRICTION COMMUNITY

F OR THOSE WHO prefer to live in the same level as they, without being disturbed by kids or teenagers, places like Sun City or Sun Lakes in Arizona can be ideal. The cost of living here is still affordable. No extra expense to shovel snow.

CHAPTER XIX

BEST STATE TO RETIRE IN

HAVING MAPPED OUT the different states, by now we must have an idea of which states are best as far as tax savings are concerned as cited above. The next question is if and when we are ready to retire.

An article appeared in the internet which gave 8 signs when it's time to retire. Customarily, people retire at 65 because it is mandated by social security requirement, the earliest available at lower benefit being 62. Those who prefer to work longer to get the maximum benefit are forced to distribute their IRA at age 72 ½.

CHAPTER XX

EXISTING ONLY, NOT LIVING

IN MY HUMBLE opinion, especially for the self-employed, it is time to retire when I am no longer interested in living; for working is vital part and parcel of living, and living without working, even on part time basis, means I am only existing; and therefore I am not living my dreams when I was young, to retire in style.

The principal reason I feel the need to retire is when I am no longer able to work because of disability or infirmity. In other words, I am happy to die with my boots on, God permits. Of course I also need to consider the other compelling reasons to retire: to spend more time with my family; to take a badly needed vacation, see the world if possible; but most important of all is if I have saved enough money to last me a lifetime.

How much is enough is the $64 dollar question. And this is when the need to see a Certified Financial Planner becomes a part of the equation in retirement. As a rough guideline per the advice of some financial planners, we estimate our one year expense multiplied by 20 or 25, and this will probably put us in a safe ball park where we don't outlive our money.

The big risk here is if we live to be a hundred as many retirees live longer now with the increasing improvement in medical science and living condition. This takes into consideration our social security income, investment income, IRA, and other sources of income which we must withdraw at the right time to get the maximum benefits. It is important to note here that although Roth IRA is tax free on distribution, the Traditional IRA, which is taxed on withdrawal, grows faster than the Roth IRA.

Another good news is that as long as we are working, we can continue to keep adding to our IRA past the old limit of 70 ½. Any question pertaining to retirement planning and income distribution will best be answered by a Certified or Qualified Financial Planner.

With our dreams come true, promises fulfilled, lives well lived, and our Estate Planning well drawn and in the hands of our successor or successor trustee, onwards to our tombs we keep on marching.

It is a well-known fact that we all go this way, but not everybody approaches or reaches his/her destiny the same way. Some just peacefully go to sleep and never wake up. I remember our neighbor who, after enjoying the celebration of her 103rd birthday, with the usual P100,000.00 gift from the Municipal government to every resident who reaches the centennial mark, went quietly to sleep and never woke up the next morning. Some just quietly disappear or drop dead. Others linger for a while in the hospital with tubes in different parts of their bodies; in care homes or nursing homes.

As nobody can ever rehearse jumping off the Golden Bridge or practice dying to meet our Creator, the next best thing to do then is to ask forgiveness for all the hurtful things we have done in life and be prepared with our bags packed; so that when the next flight comes by and we hear the church bells ringing, we know "for whom the bells toll," and we lay our open cards on the table without trepidation and without making a sudden turn around to double check if we have closed the garage door.

This ends our journey from womb to tomb.

BIBLIOGRAPHY

T HERE IS NO bibliography in the usual format being presented here because most of the information used here is from stock knowledge learned or acquired from years of schooling, reading books and the News Papers, watching TV, listening to the Radio and Religious Instructions; personal experiences and observations of others, and the Internet with Goggle, etc.

THIS BOOK LAUNCHES its opening salvo with a frontal assault on abortion in defense of the unborn. It defines life as a sacred creation of God and must be preserved at all cost and any circumstance. It asserts that to terminate pregnancy at any stage by abortion is murder of an innocent baby, a human being to all appearances.

It offers adoption as an alternative to abortion and suggests ways to facilitate the process of adoption. It follows up our different ways of living, the decisions we have to make, etc. from inception to the end of life.

In passing it dwells lightly on early childhood recollections and talks about some survivors of abortion. It also highlights some laments to old age; some discussions on ways to prepare for a happy retirement, citing the importance of financial or fiduciary planners; and lists down the pros and cons of the different states as a guideline to facilitate the decision where to retire.

Finally, this book reminds us of the best preparation for our exit from this world to the next.

Figure 7 the Author and his partner in life, Chita

ERNESTO SR. WAS born in Tagoloan, Misamis Oriental, Philippines April 10, 1931 of Chinese and Filipino parentage. After graduating Valedictorian from St. Mary's High School in his home town, he finished his Medical Degree at the University of the Philippines in 1958.

He finished his surgical training at Cambridge City Hospital, Cambridge, Mass.; St. Mary's Hospital in Rochester, N.Y.; and chief residency at the Missouri Baptist Hospital in St. Louis, Mo. in 1965.

He practiced his profession for six years in Cagayan de Oro City and Makati Medical Center, Philippines before returning to the U.S. in 1972 where he practiced Medicine and Surgery for thirty three years in Minnesota, Missouri, and Arizona until his retirement in 1996.

He is married to Concepcion C. Castro, BSE, MA, Special Ed, Truman University, Kirksville, Mo.; of Licab, Nueva Ecija, Philippines; and has two children: Amparito L. Cogswell, B.S. MBA Finance, ASU, Tempe, AZ and Thunderbird International School of Business Management; and Ernesto, Jr., M.D., MPH, Family Medicine and Occupational Medicine, Texas Medical School at Houston, and Harvard Medical School.

Printed in the United States
By Bookmasters